Gone With the Mortgage

Gone With the Mortgage

And Other Heir-Raising Stories

Jerry and Lynda Cohagan

Beacon Hill Press of Kansas City
Kansas City, Missouri

Copyright 1996
by Beacon Hill Press of Kansas City

ISBN 083-411-6243

Printed in the
United States of America

Cover Design: Paul Franitza

Cover Photos: Steve Attig

Cohagan, Jerry.
    Gone with the mortgage, and other heir-raising stories / Jerry and Lynda Cohagan.
        p.   cm.
    ISBN 0-8341-1624-3
    1. Christian life. 2. Parent and child. 3. Parenting—Religious aspects—Christianity. 4. Child rearing—Religious aspects—Christianity. 5. Cohagan, Jerry. I. Cohagan, Lynda. II. Title.
BV4501.2.C633   1996   96-2629
248.8'45—dc20   CIP

10   9   8   7   6   5   4   3   2   1

Contents

Foreword

For many seasons of concerts, Jerry Cohagan and Stephen Hicks traveled on our bus as a part of the Gaither Trio concert program, making audiences (and all of us) laugh, cry, remember, and consider those things that last forever. Bill and I have spent many a late night in truck stops with Steve and Jerry discussing world news, political developments, great ideas, recent books, the concert we just finished, or our hopes for the future. Somehow, I just never thought about the future of Jerry Cohagan in terms of being a good daddy to two precious children or a husband to an English teacher from California. But now that I see Jerry living out those two most important callings of life and doing it so well, I know that homemaking is where he was heading all along and Lynda is the person we all prayed that Jerry would find.

During those years together and in the years since, I have listened to Jerry tell stories. Mostly they were stories—real or imagined—that were so reflective of life that they were as if he'd had a mirror *and* a tape recorder inside each of our homes and hearts. We all saw our own attitudes, heard our own words, and felt our own absurdities. (How did he know?) And because he made us laugh, we were able to take a step back from the mirror, listen to the recordings, and then tackle the flaws that had been revealed in ourselves in the healing light of humor.

Now, together, Lynda and Jerry are telling stories again—this time about their kids! And this book, like the other stories, is much, much more than a collection of cute kid incidents; it is a collection of universally true glimpses at a family in process. And again, the stories are about us all, in the end, and reflect our own triumphs and failures as parents and human persons.

It is right that Jerry and Lynda tell stories. Story has always been the medium for painting the truth. Story carries the content of a culture. Story preserves the heritage of history. Story projects the possibilities of the future. Whether the family of man has gathered around a primordial campfire, hovered around the opening of a nomadic tent, squatted on the bank of a river, gathered in a country farmhouse, collected at the Grange Hall, sat on city park benches, or met at the mall over a cup of gourmet coffee, it has been the story that defined our family, community, or national identity.

The greatest storyteller of all time wrapped the Truth that *He* was in story. He would gather some folks on a hillside or a dusty road or in a city marketplace and say something like this: "A man had two sons . . ." or "A farmer went out to sow seed . . ." or "A woman lost a valuable coin . . ." When the Walking Story ascended to His Father in heaven, His final parting words to those who stood gazing up to heaven were: "Go. Tell."

Jerry and Lynda are telling as they go the story of life in the house—oh, and in the car, on planes, at school, on the stage. They are preserving a heritage and shaping identity and projecting hope. My wish is that one day their children will have remembered the story and will start to tell it to their children. Maybe Jerry and Lynda will someday receive as a gift from their children some words similar to the ones our grown children wrote and sang a couple of years ago for us all to celebrate my mother's homegoing:

And the stories make me know I'm going somewhere—
And they tell me of the ones who brought me here—
And I want to tell my children how the memory lives on,
That life will bring them love and joy and tears.
Yes, life will bring them love and joy and tears.
Stories . . . *

Oh, and Jerry and Lynda, I'm sending you a six-pack of root beer because I loved this book so much. You two can drink it some night when, instead of feeling warm and fulfilled, parenting leaves you with a lonely, hollow feeling and you wish to God you had some answers. And take it from Bill and me: even on those days, parenting, loving each other, and serving Jesus are the most important things you'll ever do!

—*Gloria Gaither*

*By Benjamin Gaither, Amy Gaither-Hayes, and Suzanne Jennings © Copyright by Townsend and Warbucks Music. All rights reserved. Used by permission.

Preface

When we first considered the idea of putting together a book from the articles we had been writing about our children over the past five years, we thought, "Why? Who would read it?" After all, stories or amusing anecdotes about your children are cute only because they are just that—*your* children. Who would want to read about *our* kids? Their grandparents, for sure, but that would only guarantee selling four copies. And we knew that any marketing department would have a larger audience in mind.

Then we began to remember all those stories we'd heard about our friends' kids—for instance, the one our good friends, Larry and Gigi Campbell, tell about their girls. It seems that Jessica and Valerie, ages five and two at the time, were both watching television in the living room while their parents were in another part of the house. Suddenly Mommy and Daddy heard high-pitched screaming coming from the living room. They rushed down the stairs to find Jessica standing over the television set with an empty glass that had contained Kool-Aid while a cloud of smoke rose from the back of the set.

"What are you doing?" they exclaimed while Valerie pointed wildly at the television set, yelling, "The TV's on fire!"

Mommy and Daddy stared at the set. It wasn't on fire, but there *was* a picture of a forest fire on the screen.

Slowly contemplating the mind of a five-year-old, Larry asked Jessica, "Did you pour your glass of Kool-Aid in the TV?"

Jessica, proud of her distinguished firefighting skills, held up two fingers and answered with a gratified expression, "Two glasses!"

We chuckle every time we hear that story. And we don't seem to tire of hearing it. After all, their stories are ours. And our stories are yours too. It is the stories that unite us, that teach us that we are not so different from each other. For, after all, the things that have made us laugh at *our* kids have made you laugh at *yours.* We cry over the same griefs; we worry over the same concerns. And so it is in the telling of the stories that we are reminded that we are not alone. Our parents told stories of us, we tell stories of our kids, and our kids will tell stories of their kids.

And it is good that we continue to tell the stories. That is how we mark our journeys. Some of our favorite Bible stories are those in the Old Testament in which people are gathering stones and building altars to mark the places where God met them on their journey. Jacob built an altar to mark where he had wrestled with the angel. Joshua built an altar after crossing the Jordan into Canaan.

And so we, too, build altars. Only ours are made of words, not stones. And so we offer to you these verbal altars—markings of where God has met us. They are markers that remind us that God is ever present in our lives—even in the small stuff.

By Way of
Explanation . . .

   Most of these pieces were written from 1991 to 1994, chronicling the first four years of our venture into parenthood. We've divided them into three sections—HIS, HERS, and OURS. We've done this for several reasons: to help you discern who wrote which articles, to allow you to give credit where credit is due, and to let you know whom to file the lawsuit against if you are offended.

OURS

A Heritage
in the Making

*S*everal years ago B.C. (before children), we opened our home to a 19-year-old in need of a safe place to live. For nine months she occupied the spare bedroom and the hall bathroom and changed our lives forever. Shelby had been through a chemical-dependency treatment program and was not welcome back into her family home. She just kind of landed on our doorstep. Actually, months later we began to realize that God had put her on our doorstep, not just because we had the room in our home, but because He needed the opportunity to remodel some rooms in our hearts.

We learned a lot in those months that Shelby lived with us. As she and her therapist began to uncover and deal with childhood abuse, we learned to thank God for our own childhoods, which were free from fear. As Shelby slept night after night with her closet light on, we began to realize that God is indeed the Light. We learned that He does provide comfort, sometimes tangibly in the form of louvered closet doors that let just enough light through to cast a safe, warm glow. Sometimes the comfort of God came more intangibly in the form of wisdom to answer Shelby's questions.

Throughout those months we began to learn a great deal about family. Not only were we expecting our first child, Chase, but also Shelby's comments about her own upbringing forced us to solidify what we wanted as we prepared to build a family of our own.

15

One Wednesday night Shelby attended an informal church service with us. As the leader directed, we looked up numerous passages of Scripture and read them aloud that night. In the car going home, Shelby asked, "How did you know where all the stuff in the Bible was?" Where all that "stuff in the Bible was" had been such a basic part of our early education that we couldn't put a finger on exactly how we knew it. After stuttering around for a few seconds, we found ourselves rolling down the highway singing the Bible song to Shelby—you know, the one that lists the books of the Bible. We learned then that Shelby didn't even have a Bible of her own and couldn't remember her parents ever reading one, even though her family never missed Sunday Mass. We began to realize that we wanted our child to know "Jesus Loves Me" as well as he'd know his ABCs. We wanted our child to know that Christ loved and cared for him and could be his best Friend, not just someone you pay homage to on Sundays in order to "play the game of religion," as Shelby would say.

On another night we attended a church dinner with Shelby. On the way home came another telling comment: "Did you notice that family that sat at the table behind us?" To tell the truth, we hadn't noticed. We couldn't remember who sat at the next table. But Shelby noticed. She continued: "They talked to their kids." We waited for her to go on, to make some point about the family. Then we realized that she had made her point—*they talked to their kids.* We didn't know whether to laugh or cry, but we knew one thing: We would talk to our kids. And listen. And laugh. And cry. And hug. And talk some more. Shelby was a daily reminder to us of how blessed we were.

Now, several years later, we keep in touch with Shelby as she continues to rebuild her life. We keep in touch with Shelby more for our own sake than for hers, because she is a reminder to us of the pledge we made to our children, forged by our experiences with her:

Dear Children,

May you always know these things: Your father loves your mother, and your mother loves your father, and we both love God and want His will. There is nothing you can do that will take our love from you. Although you may not have every-thing the world values, we will do everything to teach you that which has eternal value. When the world seems buffeted by the winds of change and discontent, may home always be a safe harbor for you, where love and mercy and laughter abound.

Flying High

In the summer of 1991 we were fortunate enough to attend our church's International Laymen's Conference in Nashville. We thought it would be a great opportunity to show off our 11-month-old boy, Chase Wesley, to all our friends we hadn't seen since the last laymen's conference. This was a pretty important milestone in Chase's life, since it would be his first airplane trip.

Lynda didn't decide to go until the last minute, so she was booked on a flight through Memphis. Since Jerry had the direct nonstop flight, it only made sense that Chase would go with him. "A bumbling man with a baby will always get plenty of sympathy help from the flight attendants anyway," Mommy replied.

"No problem," Daddy assured Mommy. "It's only an hour flight. What could go wrong? Besides, it'll give us a chance to do some bonding."

So, armed with Dr. Dobson's latest child-rearing manual under one arm and Chase under the other, Daddy confidently swaggered down the jetway. A half hour into the flight, at 33,000 feet, Chase didn't have male bonding on his mind. The only thing he did have was a full diaper. And the only thing Dobson came in handy for was to fan the air around Chase. Maybe nobody'll notice, Jerry thought. But it's pretty hard not to notice 12 arms adjusting 12 air vents directly at you. Putting on his best forlorn look, he called an attendant. The attendant smiled sweetly and said, "What a precious baby! How can I be of assistance?"

Looking as stupid as possible (which comes rather easily), Daddy said, "My boy needs to have his diaper changed."

The attendant's smile immediately became a thin, compressed line as she slowly raised one arm and pointed to the rear of the aircraft with the finger of doom and announced in a voice that must have dropped two octaves, sounding much as you would imagine the pronouncement of the end of the world, "The bathroom is in the back." So much for the "sympathy help."

Grabbing the diaper bag and child, Daddy stumbled toward the back of the plane, smiling at some very unhappy, downwind fellow passengers. "Sorry—it's his first flight—must be the air pressure."

Although air travel is quicker than the automobile, driving does have its advantages—the most obvious being that you can pull over and stop when a problem arises. Not so at six miles above ground. Also, it's a known fact that there is more square footage in the glove compartment of a car than there is in an airplane bathroom. It's a great enough challenge just trying to turn around and shut the door without hitting your elbow on the other side of the room, let alone change a baby's diaper. Add to that a guy with size-12 feet, and you can imagine the difficulties. Comparably speaking, a camel going through the eye of a needle begins to look like pretty easy stuff.

Suffice it to say that by the time Daddy came staggering out of the jetway in Nashville—Chase hanging limply underneath one arm, Dobson relegated to the bottom of the diaper bag being dragged behind him—Chase felt great; Daddy was the only one whimpering.

Mommy, looking refreshed, stood ready to greet the troops.

"How'd the 'bonding' go?" she asked, with just the slightest knowing smirk.

"Fine. Just fine. No problem, why do you ask?" Daddy growled rather defensively while swiftly depositing a much lighter Chase in his mother's arms.

Once we actually got to the church conference, everything went pretty much as we planned. What a wonderful time of coming together with old friends and making new ones! Little three-minute reunions went on all week long as we kept running into folks we knew. They would all "oohhh" and "ahhh" at our beautiful boy while Chase behaved like a "Precious Moments" greeting card. And whenever a problem did arise, Daddy could hand the 25-pound problem over to Mommy.

You could hear snatches of conversations all over Opryland: "I know your mother's sister! . . . How many kids do you have now? . . . How's Uncle Charlie's back? . . . Remember Lois from college? . . . When did you move to Phoenix? . . . No! I hadn't heard that. . . . What a beautiful baby! Was it his first flight? . . . Well, let me tell you about it . . ."

It's easy to start viewing the world as very small when several thousand people from all over the country can come together in the same room in a matter of hours. Air travel does have its advantages. Or maybe the world seems smaller when you run into so many people who are in some way connected to you. And in the midst of 3,700 family members in Nashville, we realized the blessings of a family who cares and loves—who takes the time to fuss over your baby, who takes the time to listen to your stories, who takes the time to tell you that you make a difference in their lives, who takes the time to go out for coffee to continue conversations five years old. And there is something more going on here than just old college chums and friends of a friend of a friend. There is a tie that binds us in the family of God. And maybe it's not such a small world after all; maybe we're just part of a much bigger family than we ever imagined.

Wal-Mart and Mercy

Our son, Chase, had just recently celebrated his second birthday. One of the more distinctive characteristics he inherited from his mother is his ability to carry on conversations, even if no one else is there.

We've marveled this past year at our son's language development, and most of the time we can even understand him. Of course, there are those moments when he's repeating something for the umpteenth time (such as "Nileoleum! Nileoleum!" as he stomps his foot for emphasis) while Mommy and Daddy stare at each other with a stupid, blank look on our faces. Chase eventually sighs and toddles off, shaking his head at our utter lack of comprehension. (We finally figured out that he was referring to the kitchen floor, which is, of course, linoleum.) Most of the time, though, he comes through loud and clear—emphasis on the loud.

One of his favorite words is "sawee" (sorry). We have to admit that he didn't learn it from us, though. He learned it from his best pal, little Gordie, who has a penchant for throwing things at Chase's head. He's got a pretty good aim, so Gordie's mother spends most of her time saying to Gordie, "Tell Chase you're sorry," upon which Chase quickly says, "Sawee," while Gordie usually attempts just to hug Chase, which usually leads to a wrestling match, which usually leads to "Sawee" again. At any rate, Chase says sorry now anytime he bumps into a kneecap, a chair, a table leg, a door, or a wall. He does this quite frequently, as he is overinflated by about 10 pounds.

Another favorite word is "Gabessue" (God bless you). This follows any sneeze he hears, even his own. It also follows a cough, the blowing of a nose, a belch, the clearing of a throat, or a dog barking.

And then there is "Moosee!" (Mercy!). He learned this from his mommy. "Mercy" is her all-purpose word to express surprise or consternation, as in "Mercy! That's terrible news!" or "Mercy! When will this humidity let up?" The occasion in which Chase has heard this word the most is when he's lying prone on the changing table. Invariably, what escapes Mommy's lips is "Mercy!" as in—well, you get the picture.

For a few weeks, every morning when we'd open his bedroom door, Chase would greet us loudly, exclaiming, "Wamart! Wamart!" (Wal-Mart). We're not sure why he was saying this; we're just glad he wasn't saying something like "Saks" or "Dillard's."

And then there's a word that has heralded some of Chase's masterpieces of modern art: "mess." This is proclaimed on a daily basis, mainly at mealtimes after he grows tired of eating his vegetables and finds it much more fulfilling to smear them on his tray or to hurl them onto the "nileoleum"—or right after Mommy has unfastened his diaper and exclaimed, "Mercy!" He is quick to proclaim, "Mess!"

If we all had to go through life with only a half dozen words or so, these aren't bad ones: Mess, Mercy, Wal-Mart, Sorry, and God bless you. And it won't be any time at all before Chase is waxing poetic in full-blown sentences. But before that happens, his parents wish to freeze this time and remember the lessons he has taught us in his simple exclamations:

(1) If you make a mess, call it a mess.

(2) Be generous with your mercy. A fair share of mercy makes messes that much easier to clean up.

(3) As for Wal-Mart, get out of the house now and then—either that or Chase wants us to buy American.

(4) Be willing to say you're sorry a lot, even if it's not your fault.

(5) Say "God bless you" to at least one person a day. If that's too uncomfortable, start with a dog and work up.

Thanks for the lessons, Chase. We're learning.

The Presents That Last

A few summers ago one of the projects we wanted to accomplish was editing down into a short, entertaining, fast-moving, set-to-music program the hours of videotape that chronicled the first two years of Chase's life. We knew we had our work cut out for us when we found ourselves falling asleep watching our own beloved child! In the final analysis, we settled for just the short part.

After all, how fast-moving could the video be when Chase didn't walk until he was 15 months old? And how entertaining can hour after hour in a baby swing be when it's interrupted only by a few brief forays into squash or beets dribbling down a chin? We gave up on the set-to-music aspect when we couldn't figure out the "audio dub" feature of our camcorder.

Although we'll never win $10,000 on "America's Funniest Home Videos," we did rediscover a few precious moments that we'll cherish forever. Recorded for the sake of posterity is Chase's first Christmas. While we took turns opening our gifts to each other, Jerry would reach over to Chase, who was surveying the whole scene from his baby seat, and stick the bows to Chase's head. He was six months old and laughed out loud at the rattle of wrapping paper and the bright colors of the bows.

When all was said and done, it was evident that we had spent too much on Christmas. We had given each other things we had really wanted but never hoped to have. They were special gifts—so special that our credit cards kept reminding us of it for several months. But what stood out most about that Christmas was an infant Chase with bows on his head.

And it's good that that has stuck with us. You see, we have a tendency to get a little cynical around Christmas; OK, OK—a little more cynical than we usually are. Instead of experiencing a sense of peace and feeling anew a childlike sense of wonder, we're usually just plain tired. Between Jerry flying from coast to coast and eating his way across the country at Christmas banquets and Lynda juggling the shopping and the baking and the decorating while trying to get gifts into the mail on time and finish a semester of school with final exams to grade, there seems to be minimal room left in our life for yuletide joy. And now that two children have made our life even more hectic, if there ever is a free moment, we just want a nap.

We've said it before, but it's still happening: God keeps sneaking up on us—like teaching us what Christmas is really all about in the middle of summer while editing videos. He must have known we'd be too tired to learn that lesson when Christmas actually came around. But there it was in living color on the television screen—Chase with a big red bow stuck on his forehead proclaiming himself to be the best gift under the tree.

We promised ourselves then that we wouldn't forget that. Lynda resolved that she wouldn't even try to bake as many cookies as her mom always did (and still does), and Jerry vowed that it really wouldn't matter if he didn't hang all the outside lights so our house would be as gorgeously decorated as the neighbors' (not that it ever is). Instead, we promised ourselves that we would do only the really important stuff, like rocking Tori while we sing Christmas carols and letting Chase hang ornaments on the tree (it's OK if the top half is bare). We promised each other to teach our children that Christmas is not about presents, but about the gift of the magi. It's not about tinsel and glitter, but about a star shining over a stable. It's not about a fat man in a red suit guiding reindeer, but about a babe in a manger guiding shepherds toward a glimpse of glory.

And in turn, Chase and Tori will give us the greatest gift: Christmas incarnate. They will be babes wrapped in swaddling clothes (or blanket sleepers) proclaiming to us that God still sends to humankind a message of hope.

"Miz Lucky"

A few summers ago we had some unbelievably nice August days—very un-Kansas City-ish. The evenings were cool and balmy. And night after night the Cohagans could be found sitting in the driveway in our Wal-Mart web chairs with our next-door neighbors sitting in their Wal-Mart web chairs, watching all the kids play up and down the sidewalk. Sometimes Jerry and Tom (the neighbor) would fantasize themselves as the next Michael Jordan and Charles Barkley while shooting some baskets amid dodging bikes and trikes and big-wheels. The emphasis here is on fantasy, because neither one of them would actually get up out of their web chairs to shoot. But mainly we just sat and visited and took turns treating each other to Dove bars while we waved to other neighbors passing by. We think web chairs in driveways are the next big trend—you know, the front porches of the '90s.

It was a wonderful time, when kids' squeals mixed with grown-up laughter. But it was August, and Lynda would have to start teaching soon, and always in the back of our minds was the nagging question: Who will watch our kids on days when Jerry is out of town? You see, our day-care situation is pretty odd. Because of Jerry's occupation, we need a sitter only when Jerry flies out of town on a weekday, and that's only four or five days a month. It's really hard to find someone you trust to take children on such a sporadic schedule. To make a long story short, we had investigated several options and had found nothing we were really comfortable with. And the first day of school was getting closer and closer.

We were really starting to panic, but we continued to sit out front in the evenings. One of the neighbors we had been waving at was a diminutive elderly lady who took her evening walk about the same time we'd be eating our Dove bars. One night she happened to stop and ask if she could hold Tori for a moment. While Tori giggled with delight, Mrs. Luedtke shared a little of herself with us. She had moved from Ohio a year before and lived with her daughter's family just five houses up the street. She had been widowed 20 years earlier and had spent those 20 years baby-sitting. She talked to Chase and "gootchee-cooed" Tori, and after she went on down the street, we glanced at each other but didn't say anything.

We continued to investigate daycare alternatives for the next few days, but to no avail. Unbeknownst to each other, we both just couldn't get Mrs. Luedtke out of our minds. One evening shortly before school started, we sat down and weighed our options. Almost in one breath, we turned to each other and said, "What about Mrs. Luedtke?" It was such a rare phenomenon—having had the same thought at the same time—that we knew it wasn't our own doing. We knew great minds think alike, but we also knew that didn't apply to us. It had to be God's prompting. So, on Mrs. Luedtke's next walk, Lynda offered her a seat in her web chair, and Jerry offered her his Dove bar. (A real sacrifice for him, because it was *crunchy cookie,* no less!) We talked with her some more, and needless to say, she was our answer. Our sporadic schedule suited her just fine; it was just enough to give her a little structure to her weeks.

That year we couldn't have dreamed of a better arrangement. She would come to our house at 7:30 A.M. and feed the kids while Lynda prepared to leave for school. And when Jerry flew home, he was always greeted with smiles all around and the latest creation Mrs. Luedtke and Chase had made from crepe paper, crayons, and glue. At the end of the day Chase always gave Mrs. Luedtke a huge hug and kiss when she left and would stand at the door and wave good-bye to her, saying, "Take care!"

We tend to be rather skeptical at times about God's concern for the little things in our lives. Oh, we know He has fearfully and wonderfully made us, and we know He has carefully planned our salvation. We seek God's will in our lives, but sometimes we still doubt whether He really cares about those day-to-day concerns. Mrs. Luedtke proved to us once again that God really is concerned about those day-to-day concerns. He does answer daycare prayers. He wants us to call upon His name for the sake of our children. And we learned another really important lesson: God never hurries, but He is never late.

Truly, Mrs. Luedtke was one of God's many blessings to us. And so we say, like Chase says in his nightly prayers: "God bless Miz Lucky."

Road Trip!

These two words probably strike more fear and trepidation among parents with toddlers than any other words known to humankind: road trip. They're right up there with "The principal called today . . ." and "Are you sanctified?"

Before we had our two kids, we watched our married friends who had little rug rats shake uncontrollably while their eyelids twitched without reason whenever these two words were mentioned. We used to wonder what the big deal was. Well, 10 hours, 2 suitcases, 3 shoulder bags, 2 diaper bags, 1 box of Kleenex, 1 six-pack of apple juice, 1 "special" pillow, and a box of Wet Wipes later, we, too, join the ranks of eyelid-twitchers.

Our trip was to be a simple little jaunt of five hours up the interstate to celebrate Jerry's grandfather's 90th birthday. His folks were going to be there as well, and we thought it would be nice to get some pictures of four generations of the Cohagan clan. To make matters even easier, we decided to leave the evening before and drive most of the way and spend the night in a nice motel. As we pulled the van out of the driveway, all was bliss. Chase, at two and a half years old, was locked in his car seat behind Daddy, clutching his "special" pillow and excitedly saying, "I going to Neveraska!" while Tori was in her seat next to him giggling and smiling angelically.

We don't know—maybe it's something to do with interstates—but the second we started down the entrance ramp of I-35, the imp of road trips hitched a ride with us. It started innocently enough with Chase tapping out a rhythm to go along with his 20-minute chant of "I going to Neveraska!" by kicking the back of Daddy's seat. After several requests, he stopped—but just long enough to notice that Tori was asleep. Maybe he didn't want her to miss anything, but Chase proceeded to swing his "special" pillow and hit Tori in the face, which, of course, didn't sit too well with her. She proceeded to let out a high-pitched scream that has been known to open our garage door. Mommy quickly reprimanded Chase, who said, "Sowee, Towi." "Sowee" wasn't enough in Tori's mind as she continued to trumpet her anxiety in Mommy and Daddy's ears. Chase obviously didn't care for her wailing either, and since he knew better than to hit her with his pillow, he proceeded to smack her with his hand and yell, "Stop kwying, Towi!" which only increased the decibel level of both our little angels. About the time things settled down, Chase would reach over and smack Tori again.

Since Daddy was driving (he's no dummy), Mommy had to deal with all this. And for the next three hours she did. At one point she sat between them. At another she and Tori sat in the very back seat of the van, leaving Chase free to kick Daddy's seat while Daddy tried to drive with one hand and futilely reach around with the other to swat Chase's leg away. That only served to heighten the game in Chase's mind.

Since Tori showed no signs of stopping her aria, and it seemed more important that Daddy keep both hands on the wheel, Mommy eventually ended up leaving Tori in her car seat in the back—but not before turning it around so Tori's howls were only at the moon through the rear window. This way Mommy could at least hear herself howling at Chase to stop kicking Daddy's seat!

It was at this point in the trip that Daddy eloquently uttered the maxim found in some defective gene in all fathers: "Do I have to stop this car?" It's been said through the ages and can even be read in hieroglyphics on cave walls: "Do I have to stop this dinosaur?" It can be found on scrolls in the Mideast: "I'll stop this chariot right now if I have to!"

About 10 minutes from the motel, our fiendish hitch-hiker must have gotten bored with his victory, because both our cherubs were in deep REM sleep. And two weary road warriors whose faith had sorely been tested finally pulled into the motel.

The next day we smiled as Chase pushed toy cars among the legs of octogenarians and Tori was passed from one age-spotted hand to the next. We watched how life comes full circle: one generation passing on to the next the importance of family. We live in an age where families are increasingly spread out, often separated by thousands of miles—if not the geographic kind, then the spiritual kind. Those miles we'd come seemed pretty insignificant compared to the light in our nine-month-old's eyes as she sat blissfully on the lap of her 90-year-old great-granddad. And the decibel level of our trip diminished to a whisper next to Chase's giggles as his great-granddad found all his ticklish spots. Was it worth it? You bet! We've got the snapshots to prove it.

Becoming Real

We'd just gotten the kids into bed for the night—again—after story time, bathroom, and prayers; then drinks of water, leading to another trip to the bathroom, and finally ending in fetching their favorite stuffed animals for the night.

Chase went to bed feeling a little sick to his stomach that particular night. It was no wonder. We found the half-empty tube of "soothing citrus Blistik" with teeth marks all over it under his bed. Daddy muttered, "At least his throat won't chap." Earlier in the day Tori had discovered that charcoal briquettes were edible. Imagine that—a new food group. Well, for the moment the house was quiet. And while Mommy graded a few papers, Daddy wandered listlessly around the house stepping on marbles and picking up stray Duplos. About the time we crawled under the covers, it began.

Chase decided to heave his supper all over his bed. About the time we got him cleaned up and calmed down, Tori decided it was her turn. This went on back and forth all night. But the worst of it was that by morning we were *all* sick.

So at 8 A.M. all four of us trudged into the doctor's office with varying degrees of fevers, sore throats, and runny noses. The doctor just smiled pitifully at us while envisioning that weekend in Bermuda he could now afford. We knew things were bad that week when Chase starting reminding us that it was "time for medicine." Don't you wish Sam's Wholesale Club sold amoxicillin by the gallon?

Needless to say, the house was neglected for the time being. Tori no longer colored in her book with crayons. Instead, she discovered how to make designs in the dust on the coffee table. When she'd finish, she'd look up through watery eyes and proclaim, "Pretty, pretty!" It wasn't.

We started thanking God for the VCR, because it bought us 30 minutes of uninterrupted rest. But toward the end of the week, we flopped down on the couch beside Chase and Tori to watch *The Velveteen Rabbit*. All four of us were sneezing, coughing, blowing our noses, and whining. Tori was dripping juice from a tippy cup onto the floor just so she could wipe it up with a Kleenex, and we didn't even care. Lynda looked at Jerry and said, "Finally—someone in the family who has time to clean!"

So have you ever really paid attention to that little velveteen rabbit? There's a lesson there when the Skin Horse is explaining what it means to be real:

"Real isn't how you are made," said the Skin Horse. "It's a thing that happens to you. When a child loves you for a long, long time, not just to play with, but REALLY loves you, then you become Real."

"Does it hurt?" asked the Rabbit.

"Sometimes," said the Skin Horse. . . . "It doesn't happen all at once. You become. It takes a long time. That's why it doesn't often happen to people who break easily, or have sharp edges, or who have to be carefully kept. Generally, by the time you are Real, most of your hair has been loved off, and your eyes drop out and you get loose in the joints and very shabby. But these things don't matter at all, because once you are Real you can't be ugly, except to people who don't understand."[*]

And there it was again: another reminder that even when we wonder why Chase can sing the O-B-E-Y song but can't seem to do it, or when we think we'll scream if we have to wipe one more nose, those are the moments when Mommy and Daddy are most Real.

*Margery Williams, *The Velveteen Rabbit* (Philadelphia: Running Press, 1981), 12-14.

On some days it's obvious that we are quite a bit shabbier than we used to be. A lot of Jerry's hair has been loved off, and Lynda can find graham cracker slobber on almost every Sunday dress she owns. But we are more alive, more Real than we used to be too.

And yes, those two snotty-nosed mess-makers are two life-affirming presences in our home. But they are mere echoes of the love that gives us life, for "God is love. Whoever lives in love lives in God, and God in him" (1 John 4:16). Now *that's* Real!

If your family doesn't already own a copy of Margery Williams' book *The Velveteen Rabbit,* a nice big version with beautiful illustrations, buy one for your kids, or for yourself, or for someone who has made you more Real. Tell them, "Thanks."

Garage Sale!

This past summer we held the obligatory GARAGE SALE! Here in the Midwest the garage sale is a fascinating phenomenon. You spend a week cleaning out the basement, going through closets and cupboards, pulling out everything you no longer use or want, and instead of throwing it into the trash, you stick price tags on it all, pile it onto the Ping-Pong table in the garage, and people actually *buy* it! It's amazing!

Who would have guessed that someone would actually buy a set of 12 glasses inscribed with *Junior-Senior Banquet, 1985, Point Loma College?* Or that a petite lady would offer us a buck for a broken wooden croquet ball? ("My husband's a sports fanatic. It'll make a great paperweight.") Or that a teenage girl would still buy a phone after we told her that the 3 sticks and the 0 didn't work at all. ("That's OK. It's the perfect color for my room. It'll look so cool next to my Luke Perry poster.")

It was interesting to watch each other during the sale itself. Jerry became "Slimy Sam, the Slick Salesman." If he ever wants to change careers, used cars might be just the thing. He would saunter around proffering advice on our customers' needs: "Hi there, sir! Watch a lot of TV, do you? Me too. And the best way to get in some exercise while watching is this little baby—that's right, the Thighmaster! Have a seat and give her a squeeze." Or to the mother of four: "I have a feeling those boys would just love to have a Ping-Pong table. They could play doubles for hours. And what a great baby-sitting tool too! Just lock 'em down in the basement with some Gatorade, and they won't come up until they're 18. I'll throw in the paddles at no extra cost."

Lynda, on the other hand, was the righteous moralist, subconsciously not wanting to sell a thing: "You might want to find some sleepers a little bigger. Those fit my kids for only six weeks." Or "You know, we had to actually take this Ping-Pong table apart to get it through our door." Or "Did you see that the Thighmaster is cracked on one side? Be careful—it pinches."

Chase and Tori enjoyed the event as well. Chase, who is now fascinated with pens, kept scribbling new price tags, while Tori kept picking the prices off and sticking them on herself. At one point she was priced at a mere 50 cents; fortunately, we had no serious inquiries. Jerry might have considered them.

And although there were plenty of laughs to be had as we went through our junk and passed it on to be someone else's junk for a nominal fee (we didn't purchase anything for a week afterward without paying for it in quarters and dimes), there were also some bittersweet moments. We said good-bye to the infant stage of our kids as Jerry helped load the changing table and walker into someone else's van . . . as Lynda watched ladies pick over onesies and socks so tiny that they'd fit only Chase's thumb now . . . as Mom and Dad watched a mother-to-be buy Tori's infant car seat. It seemed only yesterday that we brought her home from the hospital in it.

In cleaning out the basement, Jerry accumulated a pretty good-sized box piled with old trophies. They were mainly from college speech tournaments, with a stray Bible memorization award and a medal Lynda had received for finishing a 10K run. Knowing that no one was going to pay even a quarter for a box of someone else's trophies, Jerry toted them to the curb on trash day, tossing over his shoulder, "Let's throw them out. *Our* lives are over; we've got to make room for the kids." Lynda was taken aback. The statement seemed so casual and offhand.

But as we packed away for safekeeping more than one box of our *new* trophies—the dress Tori wore on her first day at church, Easter Sunday; the little suit Chase was baptized in; black patent leather shoes, size 0; Chase's first Sunday School "project," a blue handprint on yellow construction paper—we realized that our lives are far from over. In fact, in many ways they are just beginning. They've just been dramatically rearranged. And the shape and size of our trophies, the measure of our accomplishments, the form of our memories will never be the same.

Garage sales prove the old adage that one man's junk is another man's treasure. But Jesus' words ring even truer: "Where your treasure is, there your heart will be also" (Matt. 6:21). Our treasure is now wrapped up in two children. And a first-place trophy in a speech tournament seems insignificant next to the first words spoken by an infant son. And a medal for a 10K run pales next to the first steps taken by a sister trying to keep up.

The Great Outdoors?

Summer vacations are always a great time of fun and challenge—fun for the kids and a challenge for the parents. Last year we thought a trip to Oregon to camp and fish for a few days would be just about the closest we could ever get to heaven on earth. (All right—*Jerry* thought that.)

The voice of reason asked, "What do we do with the kids?"

"Take 'em, of course!" Jerry glibly shot back. "I want Chase to experience the great outdoors, to be one with nature."

"He's got a swing set in the backyard."

"Look—it'll be great! We'll sleep underneath the stars, live off the land, admire God's handiwork. Just think—no city lights, no noise, no phone—"

"No running water, no heat, no electricity, no indoor plumbing," added the voice of reason. "Chase'll barely be 3, and Tori'll be only 16 months old."

"I don't want them growing up thinking that Disney World and shopping malls are all there is to life." Spoken like a true mountaineer.

Anyway, Jerry wanted to play Grizzly Adams for a few days, and it seemed a small price to pay when you consider the other 360 days in the year. So for the next four months Chase would dutifully say, "We're going camping in Oregon!" without having a clue as to what he was actually in for.

Actually, it was Dad who didn't have a clue as to what he was in for. What's that old saying?—"The best laid plans . . ."

First of all, the idea of being one with nature sounded fine—until nature actually called, and Chase was not about to be one with it. This led to several hours of trying to cajole, wheedle, and coerce Chase into believing that the yellow bucket was "safe," which only led to greater frustration on the part of Dad and greater consternation on the part of son. The situation was finally relieved when Mommy stepped in and suggested to Dad, "Why don't you go 'catch' supper?" While Dad grabbed his fishing pole and stomped off, Chase gleefully hopped onto the bucket. Tori applauded and ate a handful of dirt.

Also, "living off the land" works only if the fish decide to cooperate. In Jerry's case, for the whole week the entire fish population had declared a state of fasting. And as Chase sat next to Dad and munched Oreo cookies, all Dad caught was a sunburned neck from peering down into the murky depths trying to spot some type of amphibious life form. After five days of unsuccessful angling, Chase, through a mouthful of Oreo crumbs, suggested, "I know! Let's watch *Pinocchio,* Daddy—there's a big fish in *that!*" Mom sighed and made another meal of peanut-butter-and-jelly sandwiches while Tori laughed gleefully and ate another handful of dirt.

And as far as the need for electricity went, we noticed its absence every night in our tent only when Mommy turned off the flashlight and Chase began demanding his "night-light."

Although our vacation wasn't what we imagined it would be, we did see God's handiwork. In the middle of our last night, Chase woke up Daddy and said, "Daddy, I need to go to the yellow bucket." And while Daddy groggily stumbled out of the tent holding his boy's hand, Chase suddenly froze and gasped.

"What's the matter, Chase?"

"Look, Daddy!" Chase pointed straight up to the heavens, through the towering Douglas firs to a million points of dancing, glimmering light. Chase squeezed Daddy's hand and breathlessly whispered, "God's night-lights!"

And Daddy knelt down beside his boy, wrapped his arms around God's greatest handiwork, and together they stared at the stars and cherished the moment.

Although they brought home more dirt than fish, Mommy and Daddy also brought home the memory of their little girl—dirt caked around her mouth, standing next to a gentle campfire singing "My cup is full and running over"—complete with hand gestures.

We discovered that we didn't have to go to Oregon to see God's handiwork. His blessings surround us every day in the laughter, screams, fights, hugs, and insights Tori and Chase continue to bring our way.

And this summer Jerry's been "camping" with Chase and Tori in the backyard. The facilities are better, and Jerry's caught the same amount of fish. In a couple of years we'll do the camping thing again. In the meantime, when asked the fateful question, "Lynda and Jerry, you've just survived another year of parenting. What're you going to do now?"

The reply is automatic: "We're going to Disney World!"

Gone with the Mortgage

*D*addy, what's that?"

"A duster."

"What are you doin' with it?"

"Getting cobwebs out of the corners."

"What's a cobweb?"

"Kinda like a spider web, but there's no spider."

"Do cobs live in them?"

"Go ask your mother."

Our kids have seen a whole new side to us in the last few days—we've cleaned the house! Now don't get the wrong idea. With Jerry being the live-in maid, the house stays reasonably clean and fairly picked up. That is, it's about as good as you could expect with a two-year-old, a four-year-old, and the normal amount of toys and accumulated clutter of eight years of marriage.

OK, OK—true confession: we haven't seriously *cleaned* since Chase was born and had no real intentions of doing so until after Tori started school. You know the kind of cleaning—your mom probably did it every spring: the back-of-the-closets, heaving-heavy-furniture kind of cleaning.

So here we were, virtually three years ahead of schedule, *cleaning* the house. What brought such obsessive-compulsive behavior about was an innocent call from our realtor friend who wanted to show us a house she thought we'd really like. We'd been looking at houses periodically for the past two years with no real intention of buying. Especially with the cost of new homes, we'd always come away convincing ourselves that we were just fine where we were. Our checkbook had a way of doing that for us.

Well, this particular house turned out to be everything we wanted at a price we could afford. It was our dream home. Jerry actually hadn't had the dream, but Lynda convinced him that *she* had, and that was good enough. Within a few hours we'd put down an earnest deposit, and there was a "For Sale" sign in our yard.

We leaped into action like a finely tuned instrument— Lynda, armed with mop, bucket, and mildew remover, prepared to do battle with the bathrooms, while Jerry, outfitted with putty knife, spackling, and paintbrush, attacked the walls and exterior. Chase and Tori followed us around in stunned amazement at the frenetic pace of polishing, scrubbing, and touch-up painting.

At one point Lynda grabbed the vacuum cleaner out of the closet for a quick run over the dining room carpet. (It had been a particularly crumby meal.)

Chase, wide-eyed, gasped, "Mommy, what are you doing?"

Mom answered, "I'm vacuuming."

Chase protested, "But *you* don't vacuum! *Daddy* vacuums!"

Not wanting to confuse the boy, Mommy calmly explained, "You're right, Chase—Daddy does vacuum, but I'm going to do it just this once. Daddy can do it the rest of the time." (Never too early to start sexual role inculcation.)

About this same time, Chase had been learning in Sunday School that God made the earth and everything in it. And so an interesting exchange occurred after Chase had made more trips upstairs in one day than he cared to remember to "put this Duplo in the bucket" and "put these marbles with the other ones we found behind the fridge." While Jerry was putting Chase to bed, Chase piped up in the middle of the bedtime prayer ritual and asked, "Daddy, who made that picnic table?" pointing to his Fisher-Price plastic table. Jerry answered, "I did. Don't you remember? I got out my tools, and you got out your tools, and we put it together. You helped me."

Chase, in a rather perturbed tone of voice, spoke up, "No, no, no—*God* made it. God makes *all* our toys." He hesitated a moment and then added in a thoughtful, almost disgruntled tone, "But He doesn't pick 'em up." Not bad theology for a four-year-old.

Change is good. Shock therapy, on the other hand, we're not so sure about—especially for kids aged two and four. Not knowing what it would do to the kids and us suddenly to have a spotlessly clean house that we couldn't mess up for several weeks, or however long it took to sell our home, we were absolutely thrilled when the first couple who looked at our house offered us more than we were asking. And in less than 24 hours the "Sold" sign replaced the "For Sale" sign.

As we fell into bed with sore muscles and aching backs, we realized that selling was the easy part. Moving will not be nearly as easy. And as we basked in the aroma of Old English scratch cover and Murphy's oil soap wafting through our house, we laughed and groaned and played "remember when . . ." For this was our first home—the house we were newlyweds in. The home we brought our children to from the hospital. The bedroom door where Tori decided to draw with her fork. (We erased the scratches.) The dent in the wall where Chase first realized that he shouldn't swing a bat in the house. (We spackled and painted over it.) The dining room our kids learned to feed themselves in. (We cleaned petrified milk splatters from the wallpaper.) The front flowerbeds we landscaped. (Every spring when we planted petunias around the mailbox we found JC + LC carved in the cement.)

We will take our memories with us to the new house, and we are already anticipating the memories we will make there—the first scratch on the door and dent in the wall, the first day of school, the first two-wheeler bike, the lessons God will continue to teach us through our kids. We will also take with us to the new house the Old English scratch cover. But we will not use it very soon.

Chin Up

Mommy! Tori's putting crayons in her mouth again!"

"Daddy! Tori's putting her Play-Doh in the toilet!"

"Mommy! Tori's eating her yogurt without praying!"

"Daddy! Tori dumped her grape juice on the carpet!" And on and on it goes. The past few months Chase has decided that he is Tori's personal probation officer. He follows her around just waiting for her to do something he can report back to police headquarters. It doesn't seem to matter to him if it's a major infraction, such as the time he caught her writing on the walls with a charcoal briquette, or a misdemeanor, such as Tori waving her balloon too close to what he deems to be his air space. If there's a chance she's out of line and there might be some recrimination, then it's worthy of a full verbal account to Mommy and Daddy. Actually, he's more like the gestapo than a probation officer.

But then there's the time two months ago when his watchful eye paid off. "Mommy, Daddy! Tori's standing on the edge of the bathtub!" We rushed to the bathroom just in time to watch her attempt a 180 degree pirouette and dismount with a difficulty factor of .9. OK, what really happened was that Daddy gasped and yelled, "Tori!" which caused her to lose her balance and slip and fall. Somehow in the course of her two-foot descent, she managed to hit her chin on the side of the tub and split it open. Having thoroughly rehearsed for just such an emergency, Jerry slumped to a sitting position and blubbered something about a child lawsuit. We rushed her to one of those "emergicenters" for minor injuries—you know, those "Doc in a box" places. After 45 minutes of Mommy trying to comfort Tori while Daddy huffed and puffed, blowing up surgical gloves for her entertainment, they finally got around to treating her "emergency" with four "sutures" on the underside of her chin. (The doctor informed us that they no longer do stitches. "We prefer to call them 'sutures.' It sounds less traumatic." Either way, it's still a needle and thread.)

Since then, we've watched Chase periodically ask Tori, "Show me your scar." Without a moment's hesitation, Tori proudly juts out her chin to show a faint pink line where her scar is quickly fading. We don't know who's prouder of it—Tori or Chase.

At this moment in their lives, even though Chase is only 21 months older than Tori, he's lived twice as long. It seems he somehow understands he's gained a lifetime more experience than Tori—and that, to some degree, one of his jobs is to watch out for her and protect her as best a four-year-old can. And Tori, as best she understands it, fully trusts Chase.

We see this every Sunday morning when Chase tells Tori to hold his hand while we cross the church parking lot. Fully believing that he knows best, she takes his small hand. And with Mommy and Daddy as bookends, we all troop into church. We love the fact that Chase watches out for Tori. It's cute and lovable in little kids.

But is it only for little kids? When did we, as adults, begin to let go of each other's hand? Do we have those people in our lives we look to as mentors, those who hold us accountable for our actions? We live in a society that seems to tell us we don't have to answer to anyone for our choices and actions. But among believers we know this isn't true. We are called to love one another. And one way we do that is to hold one another answerable for our choices.

We need to seek those people out in our lives, those whose wisdom and guidance can keep us from swaying from the truth. And we need to take the hand of those whose journey may not be as experienced as our own. And that requires an investment of our time, something there never seems to be enough of.

Tori has Chase. It seems he's got all the time in the world to keep her in line, to tell her right from wrong, to show her a better way to do something, to show her how to blow bubbles, to teach her how to do a somersault, to tell her to look both ways—all the time in the world to answer all her questions. To whom do you answer?

Correction and guidance never come easy. There's usually a scar or two in the process. But over time we, too, can proudly jut our chin forward and see where the grace of God through others has faded our scars away.

Idle Chatter

*E*ven at the tender ages of two and four, Tori and Chase already know where the best chairs in the house are at suppertime. You see, only two of the four chairs around our kitchen table have a view of the television set. And seeing as how the "Mighty Morphin Power Rangers" comes on just around suppertime, it's not unusual to see Tori and Chase high-kicking, karate-chopping, and morphing their way toward those two chairs.

Thoroughly versed in Dr. Dobson and knowing the dangers of TV, we have mandated an 11th commandment: "No TV during meals." Instead, we talk about our day. Now with a two- and four-year-old, this is covered relatively quickly. So one night recently, as opposed to Chase and Tori wolfing down their vegetables so they could run back to the evils of Lord Zed, Lynda held them captive around their broccoli spears (Jerry included) with the story about how their great-granddad held a robber hostage with a screwdriver to the throat in his little corner market in the 1920s.

This past Thanksgiving we had another little but delicious taste of storytelling around the table. Relatives were gathered for the usual eat-yourself-into-oblivion ritual. Somehow the conversation turned toward hunting. (The very best mealtime topic, wouldn't you say?) At any rate, there we were, listening to Jerry wax poetic about his "first kill." You have to cut him some slack; he grew up in Wyoming—*everyone* there hunted.

Apparently, Jerry's first hunting outing at the age of 14 wasn't quite the same as Jeremiah Johnson's. "OK, there I was in the cab of the pickup riding shotgun with my brother, Roy, driving. We're in the middle of a blizzard, I've got two pairs of pants on, long johns, hiking boots, my army surplus coat, and my orange hunting cap with the floppy earflaps. Roy's driving about 45 miles an hour in zero visibility when he suddenly 'spots' a herd of antelope 500 yards away. 'Jump out!' he says. And I'm thinking to myself, 'Yeah, right—I don't see anything.' But then, Roy was 16 and I was the squirt trying to make my passage into manhood. So without hesitation I leapt from the speeding truck, rifle in hand, only to bite the asphalt, roll, and tear up my knee. Needless to say, Roy had to rush me to the nearest hospital, while the only thing I bagged was a head cold and torn ligaments."

At this point Lynda was quick to add, "Tell the rest of it, Honey."

"There's nothing left—that's it."

"What about your mom? Tell that."

Through a mouthful of turkey Jerry muttered, "Oh, that. Well, I couldn't walk too well after that, so the next weekend Mom drove me out in the Ford station wagon."

"Yeah, that's it—go on—I love this part," Lynda said, grinning.

"Mom spotted a herd and drove up to within about 50 feet, and I rolled down my window and shot my first antelope."

Lynda cackled, "My great white hunter!"

Amid the general laughter, Jerry growled in his best Grizzly Adams imitation, "Hey! It wasn't easy riding in that station wagon with a stiff leg."

Now, of course, one good story *always* leads to another. That's how you know if you've told a good one. And pretty soon Ryan, Lynda's teenage nephew, is recounting his latest hunting feat that had occurred only days before. It seems that he was coming home from school after dark. It was not the usual uneventful trip home, as his mom found out when she got a call at work from a panicked Ryan: "Mom, come home right now. The most awful thing has happened!

Just come home!" Then he hung up. Karen immediately made the half-hour trip filled with worry. When she got home, Ryan showed her his wrecked car and informed her that he had hit a *huge* deer on the highway.

In the meantime, Ryan had told the neighbor man about what had happened. Karen couldn't quite understand the excitement with which the neighbor insisted on going back and finding the deer, but not being one to miss an adventure, she joined them as they piled into the neighbor's truck and went in search of roadkill. Once they located it in the highway median, excitement mounted as they discovered it was a 10-point buck. They loaded it into the truck, took it back home, gutted it, and shipped it off to a butcher.

By this time, Ryan's panic over his wrecked vehicle had been completely replaced by visions of a stuffed 10-point deer head on his bedroom wall. He convinced his mother to take out every single shelf in the refrigerator to store it until they could get it to the taxidermist. Guess what Ryan got for Christmas?

While we all laughed and groaned at the tale, Jerry could be heard muttering, "Hunting just isn't what it used to be."

But family is, isn't it? Sitting around that Thanksgiving table, we were inspired to keep telling stories. After all, stories tell us who we are; they give us our identity and help us mark our journey.

They may never achieve the ratings of prime-time television, but long after the frenzy of Power Rangers has passed, the stories will remain. So, go ahead—give it a shot. Turn it off and talk.

HIS

Misplacing Christ at Christmas

*T*he notion of Christ getting lost among the hustle and bustle of another Christmas season is not new. But we usually think of it happening to adults who have to their credit several years of being shoved and jostled at long check-out lines, people who have developed the reflex instincts of Mario Andretti when fighting for a prime parking space, veterans of screaming children pulling at their coat sleeves while standing in line to sit on a fat man's lap to whisper into his ear words leading to bankruptcy, or "seasoned" stamp-lickers who can still smile through clenched teeth while juggling 50 pounds of packages at the post office awaiting their turn to mail Aunt Martha her yearly supply of dried fruit and Cousin Ralph the 10-pound salami stick he insists he can't find out West.

The first Christmas I spent away from my parents was a cold winter night in 1980. That's when I recalled the first time I had lost the Christ in Christmas, several years before that. At that time I was not a "seasoned" adult, but I was already indoctrinated into the commercialization of the holidays, dazzled by the bright lights and tinsel, and hypnotized by expensive gifts dangling before my eyes—especially one particular gift.

I was nine years old and announced to my parents that I wanted a wristwatch. Actually, I gave them a choice: either a watch or a pony. And since I was pretty sure I wouldn't find a horse under the tree, I opted for a luminescent watch—pretty

cool stuff in 1966. This was before the word *digital* even exist-
ed. Now, of course, like any smart kid, I didn't want to place
any restrictions on my folks' parental duties and obligations,
so I also insisted I get a Johnny Speed sports car, which you
drove by remote control (as far as the cord would reach, that
is), some Hot Wheels racetrack gear, some monster models,
and various other junk I could use to clutter up my room.

But mainly I wanted that watch. I would no longer need
to ask Mom or Dad how long it was until "F-Troop" came on
TV. It'd be right there on my little wrist! I don't even remember if I knew how to tell time yet, but that didn't matter. I figured the watch would be symbolic of my growing indepen-
dence. So of course, I dropped all the appropriate hints. I
started showing up late for every meal a month before Christmas, complaining that it was because "I didn't know what
time it was." I'm not sure this was very effective, since Mom
and Dad knew I'd never missed a meal in my nine years of living. But I would have gone to any extreme to make it clear to
them that I really *needed* that watch.

And I expected to get it, for Christmas was the one
time out of the year when Mom and Dad always got my
older brother, Roy, and my younger sister, Terri, and me just
what we wanted. Somehow they always seemed to know.
And why should this Christmas be any different?

You see, I believed in Christmas and all that went with it:
the tinsel, the snow, the glitter of lights. The month of Decem-
ber was filled with magical moments. For several weeks before Christmas, instead of just saying grace at suppertime, we
would all sing some familiar Christmas carol first. We'd each
take turns on different nights choosing our favorite. As Christmas drew closer, Dad would bundle us up and herd us into
the Ford station wagon for his annual tour of the town just to
"oohhh" and "ahhh" at all the pretty lights. And coming home
from school was always filled with anticipation at what special treat would await us: fudge, divinity, popcorn balls, or
cookies hot out of the oven.

Putting up the tree was a family event as well. Dad always got to pick it out and set it up. Mom always got to put the star on the top limb. But what happened between the base of the tree and that star was always the creation of us three kids. Then Mom would gather us around the piano, and we'd sing "Joy to the World," "Silent Night," and all the other greats while Dad would hum slightly off-key to himself and carefully adjust one or two pieces of tinsel on the tree.

Mom always set up a little Nativity scene in the front window complete with a manger, a little Christ child, three wise men, and, of course, the obligatory donkey, cow, and lamb.

Then on Christmas Eve Dad would set us all down and read the story from Luke before we opened our gifts. Like most parents with three kids, they had no choice but to allow us to open our gifts on Christmas Eve. It was either that or spend the whole night telling us to be quiet. We had no intention of dreaming about sugar plums dancing in our heads. And just before we opened our gifts, Mom and Dad would tell us that giving was more important than receiving and that it wasn't so much that we got what we wanted, but that we remembered the greatest gift ever given to us was when Christ was born.

Thinking back now, with too many Christmases spent away from home and two children of my own, I can recall their words of wisdom much more clearly. All those memories of gathering us together whether it was to sing, decorate the tree, string popcorn, or whatever—those were moments that drew us closer together as a family than any other time throughout the year.

But this particular Christmas Eve was a little different. Somewhere among the strewn wrapping paper, glittering lights, and shiny tinsel I lost the meaning of Christmas. Now I dutifully ate the fudge, sang the songs, and listened to Dad recite the verses. But I sat about as still as someone trying to put socks on an octopus, waiting to tear into those pretty packages that Mom had taken such care in wrapping. Oh, sure—I knew that giving was more important than whatever, and that

I should be thankful for, uh, whatever. But what really mattered to me was that we get through all this ritual and tradition that Mom and Dad thought was so important so we could experience the actual receiving part.

I already had it picked out—a small blue box with a white ribbon around it, the perfect size for a wristwatch. So, of course, I saved it for last. I quickly tore open my Johnny Speed sports car, my Hot Wheels gear, and my monster models, all the time watching my brother, Roy, get that special gift he'd wanted—a Mattel Power Shop—and Terri her own Wendy Wet'um doll.

Now it was my turn. I tore into that little blue box thinking how I could act surprised and stunned to have gotten what I really wanted. Well, as it turned out, there was no need to act surprised. It came really natural. There in that little box was a piece of tin wire known as a Slinky. And for the first time in nine years I was at a loss for words. I think Mom and Dad were as shocked as I was. I don't recall just exactly how I looked, but I'm sure I didn't attempt to hide my disappointment.

The evening wore on, and while Dad helped Roy play carpenter and Mom followed Terri and Wendy Wet'um around the house with a dish towel, I sat in the den underneath the tree driving my Johnny Speed sports car back and forth into the box that contained that thing. A Slinky—I couldn't believe it! Roy was busy carving toothpicks, and Terri was busy playing baby-sitter—and I was stuck with a piece of coiled wire that's greatest talent was going down steps by itself.

I was hurt, and I believed I had every reason to be. It was the first Christmas that I didn't get what I'd wanted. What did they think they were doing? All this talk about giving being the greatest joy. How could they say that and then not get me what I'd told them to get me? And as I sat there ramming my car into that box, I managed to work myself up into a great little pout. I was quite good at it at that age; I'd had nine years of practice. And nothing the family did was going to help.

"No, Roy, I don't want to help you carve Mom a wooden spoon."

"No, Terri, I don't want to hold your doll."

"No, I don't want any more fudge. I don't wanna sing anymore stupid songs. I don't want anything except to know *why!* Why didn't I get what I'd wanted?"

And with that one sentence blurted out, I'd managed to get everyone's attention and bring Christmas to a screeching halt, kind of like fingernails down a chalkboard. Once I'd rediscovered my vocal chords, there was no stopping me. "Roy got what he wanted, and so did Terri. Why didn't I?" Mom and Dad exchanged a furtive glance. Sticking my lower lip out as far as possible, I scrooged, "This is the worst Christmas ever! I'm going to bed."

And with that pronouncement, I stomped off to my room and slammed my door plenty loud enough for all to hear, sat down on my bed in the dark, and fully expected Mom and Dad to come in any moment and tell me how sorry they were for not getting me what I'd wanted. So there I sat with my arms crossed, in the dark—waiting. No one came.

And as I sat there, I got angrier and angrier at my parents. And as much hurt pride that a nine-year-old could muster just welled up inside me until I wanted to rip my brother's GI Joe's arms off! Or stomp all over Terri's Mystery Date game!

I settled for my pillow. I grabbed it up with my fists clenched, ready to rip it to shreds, when there, underneath it, was a small green dial glowing in the darkness at me. I put the pillow on my lap, turned on my bed lamp, and reached for the card resting underneath the waterproof, luminescent watch. The card said,

Dearest Jerry:

We hope this watch will be a reminder to you of the time Jesus was born—and that the greatest gift ever given was when He laid down His life for you. Never forget that only when we give do we really receive.

Love,
Mom and Dad

I didn't go back out and apologize—I felt strangely below that. Instead, I simply buried my head in my pillow and cried. And in the darkness of that moment, a nine-year-old boy sifted through the wrapping paper, tinsel, and glitter of lights to rediscover that which he had lost.

This Christmas season, may we each take the time to find our own way back to Bethlehem.

As Sure as
Death and Taxes

Two years B.C. (before children) in the spring of 1988, while my tax accountant was preparing that year's taxes, he discovered an error he had made on the previous year's 1040. The "slight adjustment," as he deemed it, ended up costing me virtually all my savings. Lynda and I had been married for less than two years, and I was devastated to watch our "nest egg" cracked open, scrambled, and served up on a platter to a hungry Uncle Sam. Obviously, I had two choices: whine through the experience or learn from it. I did both—the latter only with Lynda's help. Oh yeah—I also dropped my tax man quicker than you could say "audit."

April 15—an indisputable, unavoidable reality. As sure as death and as certain as Rush Limbaugh with an opinion.

My mind flounders in a pool of numbers totaled and retotaled from savings accounts, money markets, certificates of deposit, and mutual funds. Any way I shove them around, they just don't total the "amount you owe" on line 65 of my 1040. And in a moment of deep commiseration with my wife, I glibly spout, "I hate my life"—great words of comfort to my life's mate.

Slowly and patiently she coaxes me away from the spreadsheet of numbers emblazoned on the computer screen. How can our whole life come down to a column of assets versus debits? Even the numbers glare back in a bright green as if to mock me as the supposed "breadwinner" of our home.

She wraps her arms around me and tries to hug away the facts. My arms hang limp. "How can you just pretend this problem doesn't exist? Life in the real world doesn't work like that. We can't just hug and play make-believe!" Angry words fired off in frustration, not at the ceiling (where they would've been better directed), but aimed dead center at the heart of the one I love.

A quiet dinner. While she silently clears the table, I continue to methodically beat the lumps out of my mashed potatoes with my spoon and gnaw at my Swiss steak as if it were the last remains of an Internal Revenue Service employee. (Tough cut of meat.)

Later on she suggests a drive about the countryside. The numbers on the screen refuse to change, so why not? I slump down on the passenger side, refusing to drive. As we leave suburbia and the sound of lawn mowers and kids playing in every other driveway, I bury myself deeper in my seat. From my vantage point I can't avoid the fact that the sky is preparing to put on an undeniably beautiful sunset. She knows better than to draw it to my attention, so she just continues to drive slowly and let the road lead us to wherever.

The kink in my neck is killing me, so I finally sit up and stare out the side window. I notice a pasture full of Holstein cows. They've all managed to stick their necks between the barbed wire to get the better grass along the roadside. Stupid, dumb animals, I think. Then I notice far off to one side of the field something else is taking place.

"Stop the car," I say. One cow is not busy chewing her cud. She stands off from the others while a small calf romps all about her, nuzzling her warm underside, then running off a few feet only to kick up its heels and then return back to its mother. These two are different. She and her newborn are not concerned with getting the best grass. At this moment in time they are concerned only with celebrating each other and playing in the spring dusk before light is gone.

I wonder if the mother knows that this moment of play is special and limited and that soon enough her newborn will grow up and take its place alongside the others who strain for what is just out of reach, cutting themselves in the attempt.

And then I wonder: who is really the stupid animal—the cow or me?

April 15 will come and go.

I reach across and rest my hand on my wife's. She entwines her fingers in mine, celebrating what is real. The sunset bursts across the sky in streaks of blue and gold, amber and wheat, demanding of me to acknowledge what is worth holding onto and what is not.

A Letter to Dad

The following are several entries from a journal I kept in 1992. My dad had just retired after having worked 44 years as a meat cutter for Safeway. Like most parents who have finally raised three kids and gotten them all out of the house, he and Mom planned on visiting each of us kids and spending top-quality time mastering the fine art of spoiling their four grandchildren, one of which was ours. In the winter of 1992 Chase was one year old.

Dear Dad,

As I descend through 15,000 feet, I glance out my window and look at Casper Mountain below me. I recall as I was growing up you used to bring me to Garden Creek at the foot of this mountain just before sunset, and we'd sit on the hood of the car and watch the deer come down into the valley to feed and drink. We never said much to each other—we'd just watch the deer and know that it was special. I don't know if we will see the deer this time on my visit home. For this trip began five hours and 1,000 miles ago as Mom called to tell me you'd had a massive heart attack.

February 10

I stand next to your hospital bed, and you tell me you have a heart pump inserted through your right upper thigh and you are not allowed to move your leg. They tell us your heart is "like wet tissue paper," and the pump allows your heart to rest. "How long can the pump stay in?" we ask. They tell us no longer than a week. Between Roy, Terri, me, and

Mom, we take turns holding your hand while you gaze beyond us, looking frightened and bewildered.

February 11

We are informed that quadruple bypass surgery will take place on Friday, February 14. Until then we are allowed to see you for only 15 minutes every two hours. And in that amount of time we try to be the strength you no longer have on one half of your damaged heart. Chris, your grandson, sends you a get-well card and writes, "Aren't you lucky? You get to have your broken heart mended on Valentine's Day." We all hope and pray for the childlike faith of an 11-year-old.

February 12-13

For the next two days we hold each other and try not to cry and spend the time between visits telling stories about you. Roy reminds me of the time we were fishing in a rowboat and you kept telling me, "Cast the other way, Jerry." Did I listen to you, Dad? Sure I did. Right after I pierced your earlobe with a No. 4 Bear Claw hook.

Mom shows us the new cabinet you built for her next to the stove. I secretly check the wood screws on the hinges, because I know of a gate in the backyard that tested your Christianity when the screws wouldn't twist to your will. Who says you can't just hammer a screw in like a nail? For years after that you kept that gate on its hinges with nails, wire, and a prayer.

I recall you and me playing golf almost every weekend for a couple years when I was in high school. You were never any good, and you were the first to admit it—to yourself and anyone within earshot. For 18 holes you would gasp, groan, agonize, invoke plagues, and mutter, "I don't know why I do this. I'm losing more balls than I'm hitting. Ain't doing nothin' but playing marbles out here!" Then as we'd load the clubs into the trunk you'd say, "Wasn't it nice and relaxing out here? Want to play again tomorrow?" And we would. I don't know which of us was the bigger fool.

Terri remembers the time you got her snow skis for Christmas. As she began unwrapping them, you were so excited to see her reaction that you actually got up and tore the wrapping paper off for her. Don't deny it—we have the snapshot. Whether it was unwrapping gifts, golfing, repairing a gate, or fishing, you were never one to sit still for long. We all smile at the memories and grow silent, each of us desperately hoping to make more.

February 14

Just before the surgery the doctor pulls us aside to tell us that because of the massive damage to your heart the prognosis isn't good and to say everything we want to say to you before the surgery and not to expect a miracle. For the next four hours we pray for exactly that. I don't know whether the angels were rejoicing, but I know that the saints in the waiting room were when the doctors wheeled you out and said they were surprised at how well you did but that the next 24 hours were critical.

Terri comes out of ICU and says, "There's 16 bottles dripping fluid into him." I count at least nine tubes entering your body.

February 17

We watch as the heart pump comes out and you are finally allowed to move your leg after seven days and the bottles of fluid, one by one, begin to be removed. The local pastor takes your hand and prays an eloquent prayer of thanksgiving. When he says, "Amen," you say, "Pastor, get me a drink of water. That prayer was so long-winded it made me thirsty." We all laugh and hug and cry some more, knowing that you're going to be OK.

February 24

As I ascend through 15,000 feet I think about the healing miracle that began 10 days ago. Looking out my window, I see Casper Mountain fading behind me. Once again, my mind sees the deer we used to watch feed. We did not make it to Garden Creek this time. But you told me yesterday that the deer were now tame enough to eat out of your hand if you offered them an apple. And together we watched the sunset from the second floor window of room 208. Once again we know it is special, made more so by the reminder that our days here are limited and precious. I sit next to your bed and take your hand. You're the first to squeeze back. I meet your eyes and see myself reflected in them. We both grip tighter, holding on for dear life. I lean over you, for I have something important to say. You already know it, but that doesn't matter. It still needs to be said. Can you hear me? Listen, Dad. Listen closely to the beating of a son's thankful heart. I love you. I love you. I love you . . .

And in the summer of 1993 I had the privilege of watching my dad take his grandson's hand and help Chase feed the deer a Dorito out of his palm. I captured the moment on video, and I will continue to pull out the tape and show Chase the moment. He may not understand the full significance of it now, but he will come to understand, because I will continue to tell him the story of how God met Grandpa and us in our need.

Father, Son, and Insect Repellent

*I*t began like any other typical day. Chase came bounding down the stairs from his room at 6:45 A.M. on the dot and began pulling the comforter off of me. "Come on, Daddy. I need bwekfas—now!" I stumbled to the kitchen and unceremoniously dumped some Cheerios and a banana into his Noah's ark bowl and headed for the shower. "Wait, Daddy! I need to pway." Oops. Through half-closed eyelids, I watched Chase fold his hands and thank God for each individual Cheerio in his bowl. By the time he reached "Amen" I was almost awake.

I love spending the days with my son. Since Lynda teaches school and my work usually is on weekends, I get to be "Mr. Mom" during the week. And I love it—most days, that is. Then along comes one of those days that makes me question again whose idea it was to have a kid. (For the record, it was Lynda's. The last big decision I made was to get married.)

About midmorning I was sitting at my computer (just like now) trying to work when suddenly I realized it was much too quiet. I hadn't been interrupted by Chase for more than 15 minutes! Something was definitely afoot. As I opened the study door I heard Chase whispering in the living room. I tiptoed to the edge of the stairs and peeked around the corner. Greeting my eyes was what looked for all the world like the testing of an atomic bomb—an enormous billowing mushroom-shaped cloud of fine white powder. At ground zero was my two-and-half-year-old boy. Kneeling, he was holding the jumbo container of baby powder upside down over his head, vigorously shaking it while whispering, "I working hard—this is good work." I'm sure he knew that he was gonna pay for his "good work," so he must have thought, "Why not go hog wild?"

When he had gotten what he considered a sufficient mound of powder piled up before him onto the carpet, he would gently set the powder down, bury his head in the mound, and blow for all he was worth. Then he'd start all over again. Needless to say, his punishment was meted out swiftly and with authority—right after I grabbed the videocamera and captured the moment. (After all, if I won the $10,000 I'd be sure to tithe 10 percent.)

About an hour later while I was still vacuuming down all the furniture and throwing open all the windows in the house, I heard a piercing scream come from the kitchen. I've learned the difference between Chase's "I'm gonna get some mileage outta this" wail and his "I'm in immense pain!" scream. This was indeed the second kind. I rushed to the kitchen to find Chase rubbing his eyes. At his feet lay a little pump bottle of insect repellent. I grabbed him up in one arm, turned the water on in the sink with the other, laid him out on his back on the kitchen counter, and shoved his face under the tap. For some reason Chase wasn't too happy with this, and he began screaming, "It's all better! It's all better!" while turning his head from side to side. Of course, I knew the water needed to go in his eyes and not his ears, so I pinned his head down between the breakfast dishes in the sink and held his eyelids open. After about 10 minutes (which felt like an eternity), Chase blubbered in my arms while a nurse tried to reassure me over the phone that I'd done the right thing.

It had been a rough morning. I decided we both needed a nap in order to regroup for the afternoon. So together we lay down on Mommy and Daddy's bed. It wasn't long before Chase was snoring deeply, not a care in the world, looking like innocence personified.

I know men can't carry a baby to term and experience whatever prenatal bonding is. But I knew that lying there next to my son, wrapping myself around him like a big C around a little c, was the closest I'd ever get. I know there will be days soon enough when I won't be able to scoop him up and wash away his hurt. And soon enough he will no longer hold his arms out and say, "I need a big hold, Daddy." So I will count these moments precious. And I will bury my nose a little deeper in his hair and smell the mischief of baby powder and insect repellent. It is in these moments that I thank God my wife talked me into having kids. Because even when it's really messy, being a dad is really good.

The Taste of Kindness

In 1966, when I was the tender age of eight, my family made a temporary move to Central City, Nebraska. My great-grandmother had had a massive stroke and was hospitalized for what turned out to be more than nine months. During this time we moved in with my great-granddad. Mom and Dad helped care for Grampa Jones and the house while we three kids attempted to adjust to this small town. Central City was, and still is, a small farming community of about 1,500 people.

Making new friends is hard enough without the added obstacle of being introduced to a new classroom halfway through the year. I stood there in my new bell-bottomed jeans and Keds while a field of overalls and feed caps stared back. I was given a seat in the very back row, where I contemplated my feet most of the time.

I remember taking my first test, and as we passed the papers forward, each person in front of me erased one of my answers and changed it. The real humiliation was not flunking the test but being unable to vocalize the injustice without being further ostracized by what I considered to be a bunch of hayseeds. They had me. I was not one of them, and they planned on keeping it that way.

There were two constants in my life during this time of upheaval. One was the train whistle that sounded its approach at exactly 4:10 every afternoon. Having no friends gave me plenty of opportunity to watch pennies get crushed, not to mention watching my GI Joe lose both his legs to the mighty rails.

But what I remember most is standing on one side of the tracks and screaming at the top of my lungs while the train rushed by me, separating me from the rest of the town. Even at eight, I found this metaphor did not escape me. I wondered, even then, how people could be so cruel. And I stared into the distance until the train and my scream were both swallowed by the cornfields.

The other constant was Kate's Root Beer Stand. Every evening toward dusk that summer, while other kids finished their baseball games or started the nightly ritual of Kick the Can, I walked three blocks to Kate's. Kate, a lady who seemed ancient to me, would always smile broadly and shout, "Why, it's Mister Jerry! Come on back here and help me make these floats!"

I'd pull over a picnic table bench and hoist myself up on the ordering window and crawl through to the other side while Kate always cackled, "Don't be gettin' stuck, or I'll have to close down for the summer." She'd hand me a frosted mug, and I'd raise it as high as I could, trying to center it underneath the lever. Then she'd pull the lever, and we'd both laugh gleefully as the stream of root beer sloshed into the mug, some of it splashing onto my face and hair.

Kate always sat with me at the picnic table, and we'd watch the fireflies and listen to the crickets lull us toward sleep. In the distance we'd hear faint shouts of "Ollie ollie oxen free!" or "Timmy, Becky! Time to come in!"

I don't know if Kate knew how lost I felt or how lonely I was, but she always tousled my hair and said, "See you tomorrow night. And don't be breakin' our date. There's nothin' worse than a woman scorned." Then she'd gently swat me on the rump, sending me on my way. I missed her terribly when, after nine months, my great-grandmother died and we moved back home.

Almost 30 years later, I have traveled much farther than the 4:10 train ever could have taken me. I've put my toes into several oceans and listened to seagulls squawk their misery at the waves. I now live where fireflies and crickets still make their presence known but are harder to find over the lights and noise of the city. I feel older but not all that much wiser.

These things I have learned. I now know that age has nothing to do with cruelty or tenderness. And loneliness and loss are never far away. Time can take pain and turn it into bittersweet memories. And root beer will always taste like kindness.

Almost 30 years later, the only changes in Central City are paved roads instead of gravel, and I've heard a rumor that there's a 7-11 on the corner where Kate's Root Beer Stand used to be. I don't want to know if it's true. But if it is, I hope she made a killing.

HERS

Kindergarten Terror

We all have moments that we look at in retrospect and say, "Something happened back then, and it was more than just what was happening." You know the kind—moments in which you were profoundly moved, or shaped, or changed. And they usually spring out of the simplest of events. I believe I had one of those moments when I was five. (When I said "retrospect," I really meant it.)

The year was 1962. I attended kindergarten at Manuel White Elementary School in Hayward, California. Like most of the kids in my neighborhood, I walked the three blocks to school each day. I walked with my friend, Anna, and we thought we were *very* sophisticated. The kindergarten classes had a special playground just for them; it had a jungle gym that looked like a horse, and Anna and I rode that horse to all sorts of places that only kindergartners can go. Sometimes Mrs. Heindel (no doubt the prettiest teacher in the whole world) would make popcorn for a snack, but even when she didn't, the graham crackers and milk were still wonderful. It was truly an idyllic existence.

It was during that year that my mom started sending canned goods to school with me. Other kids brought cans too, and Mrs. Heindel put our names on them in masking tape and put them away in a cabinet between the coat closet and the finger paints. None of this struck me as strange—after all, I had never been in kindergarten before. And you see, I did not know where Cuba was. I did not know what a missile was. I did not know what the strange triangular sign on the

side of Manuel White Elementary School meant. I had not yet
learned to read the words "Fallout Shelter." I only knew that
my mom was sending canned goods to school with me in case
the neighborhood needed to live in the school building for a
while. (Boy! That'd be fun!) Absolutely none of that was scary
to me. My parents may have worried about the Cuban missile
crisis a little, but in 1962 I had *real terror.*

Terror was two huge boxer dogs that lived in a yard I had
to pass on my way to kindergarten. These were ferocious
beasts kept at bay by a sagging chain-link fence and a very
scrawny hedge. Whenever they heard the least little sound on
the sidewalk, they would charge that fence, bare their teeth,
and growl and bark *loudly.* This terror was not the mere fig-
ment of a five-year-old imagination. We had even heard our
parents talk about how the dogs had bitten people.

To avoid this terror, Anna and I developed great strate-
gies. In the morning we walked in the company of my older
sister, Karen, and her friend Betsy. In the company of our
older "protectors" we would cross to the other side of the
street, pass the "mean dog" house, then cross back to the
side of the street we needed to be on for school. This was a
great strategy with only one major drawback: we were not
allowed to cross the street without someone older with us.
At noon, when we came home alone, Anna and I had to
stay on the side of the street with the barking boxer dogs.
And believe me—we soon mastered the art of *tiptoe.* We
could silently walk along that sidewalk, not talking, not
rustling our papers, scarcely breathing until we were safely
past "the house." Forget learning to write our names—we
were achieving far more complicated things!

The year progressed, and one day Mrs. Heindel started
sending our canned goods home with us. Most of us took
our cans home one or two at a time so they wouldn't be
heavy—but not my friend Anna. She just let hers pile up.

So there we were on the last day of school. I'm carry-
ing both Anna's papers and mine. She's struggling under

the weight of a huge sack of canned goods. We had not gone far before Anna's sack started to tear. But not being faint of heart, we continued on. Just as we were even with that "mean dog" house, the entire bottom dropped out of Anna's sack. Those two barking boxers charged that fence more ferociously than we'd ever seen as canned goods clanged and banged and rolled all over the street. We were absolutely terrified. We were trapped between canned goods in the street in front of us and dogs about to eat us alive behind us.

So we did what any self-respecting five-year-old in the same situation would do: we sat down on the curb and we cried.

Usually my dad is very absent-minded. But on this day, he realized that I had not arrived home when I should have. And he came to find us. To this day I can still feel the overwhelming relief when I saw that familiar 1960 Chevrolet Impala round the corner. He was exactly what we needed: someone bigger than the barking dogs who could step into the street without being afraid. My father picked up the canned goods from all over the street, loaded Anna and me into the car, and took us home.

I will tell my children this story because of what I have learned from it in retrospect. I want my children to know what kind of a man their grandfather is. I want my children to know that their mother has been afraid and that they will be afraid. I want them to know that sometimes it's OK to let other people pick up the pieces for them. I want them to know that sometimes the best friend they can be is one who will sit down with their friend and cry. But most of all, I want my children to know that they have a Heavenly Father who will one day gather them up and take them home.

Showers of Blessing?

Ever had one of those months that left your head spinning? In April 1992 our second child was due the first part of the month. (Just for the record, she's a beautiful baby girl named Victoria Anne; we call her Tori.) In anticipation of being the all-American family with two kids and a mortgage, we went out and bought a minivan two weeks before Tori was born.

Now that all sounds well and good until you throw in a totally unexpected hailstorm one week after the baby was born. My mother proclaimed it as the "biggest hail I've ever seen." It was the genuine article, the actual golf-ball-sized stuff. Fortunately, it didn't fall in our particular neighborhood. Unfortunately, the brand-new minivan was at the dealership getting a short in the radio repaired, and the dealership received the very worst of the hail. So there it was: a brand-new van that looked like it had lived through the looting of Los Angeles. We hadn't even made the first payment yet!

And speaking of payment, April is always a lousy month financially for us. With Jerry being self-employed, April hits us with those tax payments for the old *and* the new year. The property tax is due then too.

And speaking of due, we would lie awake night after night worrying about all the mess, not being able to turn off our minds. Just when we would relax enough to drift off, Tori would be due for a feeding. For a few weeks there, we didn't think we were having any fun at all. You know—the old "Why me?" syndrome.

But God always seems to interrupt my self-pity routines, usually like a slap in the face. Lately, though, He's been pretty sneaky about it. I'll just be going along trying my best to cope with two kids in diapers, thinking my existence is measured in four-ounce increments of Similac formula, when something breaks through the blur, comes into focus, and says with amazing clarity, "This is a blessing—cherish it."

There's the blessing of the sandbox. During Chase's "The new baby's here and I'm gonna whine" phase, Jerry bought 20 dollars of sand, came home, and dumped it into last summer's baby pool. Chase loves it. The first day, he sat out there for hours, playing in sand, stirring sand, digging sand, eating sand (he thinks it's another food group). Jerry and I were able to sit down and eat a meal in peace, enjoy each other's company, and realize there's still a marriage here and we still like it—a lot.

There's the blessing of the love pat. Chase sneaks over to Tori's cradle and peers over the edge at his sleeping sister. He stretches his arm out and pats her back while saying "Be-be" as only he can. My heart is warmed as I realize children come ready to love. In that moment I learn that if I am going to impact my world at all, I am going to have to approach it ready to love.

There's the blessing of laughter. Have you heard about the day Jerry was going to the mall with Chase? Chase was in the stroller as they entered through an expensive department store directly behind a lady in a full-length fur coat. Chase sits up, lunges forward, points to the fur coat, and yells at the top of his lungs, "Doggie! Doggie!" for as long as the lady is in sight. We think he'll probably be one of those animal rights activists when he grows up.

There's the blessing of ceremony. When Tori was five weeks old, we had her baptized. It was one of those auspicious occasions that calls for everyone to be on his or her best behavior. Surprisingly, no one was too embarrassed. Tori slept through the whole ordeal, but she looked great in the obligatory white lacy dress. Jerry even wore his one-and-only suit in honor of the occasion. And in between all my worries about possible spit-up and probable crying (of Tori, not Jerry), the words of the pastor actually broke through—another of those clearly focused moments. I realized anew that God, through His prevenient grace, reaches out to us before we are even conscious of Him. Baptizing Tori affirmed that which is truly important: we have been redeemed, and we claim that redemption for our children.

In light of all the richness of my life, things like damaged vans become mere chaff. I can look at my son's sand-caked smile or watch my daughter sleeping or see the glory of redemption in a baptismal chalice, and everything within me shouts: let it hail—I have seen a bit of heaven!

The Untold Story

Many people, when they find out our kids' names are Chase and Tori, inquire as to their origin. Actually, it usually goes something like this: "Those are kind of strange names—where'd they come from?" And my response, as well as the truth, is, "Well, I'd taught high school kids for 10 years before we had Chase, and it was the only name we could come up with that I hadn't had in my class."

In fact, when I recall the name-choosing process that we went through, it went something like this:

Jerry: "How 'bout Chad?"

Lynda: "Oh, no—not the weirdo who hid behind his hair?"

Jerry: "What about Greg?"

Lynda: "Forget it—had an insolent one two years ago."

And on it goes until you have two kids named Chase and Tori. Jerry's convinced I arrived at those names through subliminal advertising. You see, to and from school I used to drive by an office complex called Torries Chase. I reminded Jerry how lucky we were that *he* hadn't named our kids. They'd be Baskin and Robbins.

But also sandwiched between and among all those faces that have passed through my classroom are the ones that make me think, If my child turns out to be half as neat as you, I'd be a very proud parent.

As I am writing this, I have just finished my 15th year of teaching English in a public high school. As of the fall of 1995, I was in my 16th year of trying to teach 16- and 17-

year-olds the truths embodied in American literature and how to write a decent essay.

I know we're always hearing about the insurmountable problems among America's youth. And I will grant you that the world my kids will come of age in scares me senseless. I know all about the sexual activity, the drinking and drugs, the lack of respect—lives devoid of purpose or direction. I've seen invocations and benedictions disappear from high school commencements. I'm concerned about the implications of the current legislative debate regarding religious harassment.

But I also know that every year students sit in my classroom bearing the love of God in such ways that I think, If only my kids will be like you. . . . I know there are Bibles tucked in book bags and silent prayers being offered for classmates and even teachers. And as Jerry and I struggle with the difficulties of raising two strong-willed children whose gene pool is weighted heavily with obnoxiousness, the students I teach do not discourage me at all—in fact, quite the contrary. Many of my students are living testaments to the fact that God is still working, that He has not abandoned us, that love is indeed more powerful than evil.

Katy sat in the first seat of the second row. She lives with her mom, whom she doesn't respect much, but the fridge has food in it. Her brothers live with her dad, whom Katy respects more, but the fridge there is empty. No one goes to church except Katy. She never misses. Because she hasn't seen it often, she knows a stable, unshakable thing when she sees it, and it's the love of a redemptive God. During sixth hour, if we'd run across some biblical allusion in the literature that undoubtedly some of the students had never heard of, I'd turn to Katy and say, "Why don't you look that up?" And Katy would pull a well-worn Bible out of her book bag and do just that. If Chase and Tori grow up with the kind of unshakable faith in a God who "shines forever without change or shadow" (James 1:17, TLB) that Katy has, I'll be very proud.

Garrett sat alone in the last row. He is smart, good-looking, and a good athlete. He holds himself somewhat aloof from the rest of the class. The others believe he thinks he's a little better than they. He won't work in a group; he'd rather do the whole project by himself. He's "just too cool." But one day my third-hour class was discussing a story; we were talking about "the seeds of something very fine" that are in all of us. Helayna was sharing about how she didn't seem to know anymore what was fine in her. Her sharing was heartfelt and vulnerable and honest and brought tears to her eyes. When she was done, "too-cool" Garrett got up, walked over to Helayna's desk, and hugged her. The rest of us just sat open-mouthed. It was a rare thing to see such a kind, sensitive action exhibited in a 17-year-old in a public high school in front of his peers. If Chase grows up with the sensitivity of Garrett, I'll be very proud.

Amy sat in the second seat of the fifth row. Amy is continually described in the teachers' lounge as "the most solidly grounded kid I've ever met." Other teachers seem so amazed by this skinny kid with a huge heart. But I know her secret: her parents love God and serve Him and pray for her every day; her grandparents love God and serve Him and pray for her every day. And Amy loves God and serves Him and prays for her classmates and teachers every day. If Tori grows up with a heart for humanity and faith in prayer like Amy has, I'll be very proud.

And so Chase begins preschool this year, but he will not go alone. He will go with the prayers of his parents and grandparents and the legacy of countless students who have sat in Room 401 and demonstrated to their teacher that God is with us. You see, I hear a lot of shocking things in the halls, but if I really listen, there is also the sound of angels' wings.

Learning to Lean

By the time you read this I will be well into another school year, another set of 16-year-old faces who will sit in my classroom and read American literature and discuss how symbol relates to theme and all that other rigmarole that seems so important at the time. But when I was writing this, I was winding up the year, hardly able to endure the final three weeks of school in anticipation of summer vacation: days spent without a schedule, days spent on a swing set and in a sandbox, picnics in the park, or just in the backyard. It seems we spend most of our lives getting ready for something, waiting for it to happen, don't we? But we're wrong, you know. While we're waiting on it, we miss an awful lot of life.

I'm slowly learning what those writers I've been teaching for years had to say is really true. Charles Dickens wrote: "It was the best of times, it was the worst of times, it was the age of wisdom, it was the age of foolishness, . . . it was the spring of hope, it was the winter of despair." King Solomon put it this way: "There is a time for everything . . . a time to weep and a time to laugh, a time to mourn and a time to dance" (Eccles. 3:1, 4). I'm beginning to learn that this is life; it doesn't get any better than this, and it doesn't get any worse either; that the pain and healing, grief and laughter, oppression and redemption are all wrapped up together. It's one big package deal, and we need to embrace it all, to lean into it. We must face the pain so we'll recognize the healing; once we have grieved, the laughter sounds that much sweeter.

It doesn't get any worse than Jerry's friend and partner for 20 years being diagnosed with cancer, and it doesn't get any better than hearing Chase's nightly prayer: "Bless Mr. Stephen—make him well."

It doesn't get any worse than the rage you feel when your son has dumped the jumbo-size baby powder on the entryway linoleum. And it doesn't get any sweeter than the delight on his face as he looks at you and announces, "It's snowing on the linoleum!"

Several years ago I wrote what Jerry refers to as "The Quiche Thing," for lack of a better title. It is not as eloquent as Dickens, but it is a very real testimony to a desire to embrace life—all of life.

> This is a poem for my good friend Larry Campbell
>> and this is for the way he calls
>> at 5:18 on a Friday evening
>> and wants you to be thankful and poetic
>> on Sunday morning
>> less than 48 hours away.
>
> And this is for the way
>> you're in the midst of crumbling bacon
>> for the quiche for supper
>> and your fingers are greasy
>> and then the phone's all greasy
>> and you don't feel very thankful at all
>> looking at all the mess
>
> Until you realize it's a pretty wonderful mess
>> because it means
>> there'll be plenty of delicious quiche
>> to be thankful for
>> while millions wonder if there will be
>> supper at all
>> not to mention "delicious."
>
> And this is for the way you have friends
>> who call because they believe you
>> have something worth saying.

And this is for the way
>your already really fat baby
>starts howling for supper
>when there's still 12 minutes
>before the quiche comes out of the oven
>and after 7 minutes of whining
>you don't feel very thankful at all
>until 5 minutes later when
>the already really fat baby
>eats quiche and loves quiche
>(as if there was ever any doubt!)
>and laughs out loud
>and looks pretty cute
>with crumbs in his hair
>and egg on his face, literally.

And this is for the lesson learned on a Friday evening
>because I guess life is always like that—
>you can choose to see the greasy phone
>or savor the quiche lorraine
>you can choose to endure the howling
>or cherish the laughter
>'cause even when it's really messy,
>life is really, really good.

Our days are like that, aren't they?—the good, the bad, the oppressive, and the redemptive—all wrapped up in this moment or this week, or this year, or this lifetime. May we lean into it all.

Quiche II:
A Thanksgiving Celebration

*T*his is another poem for my good friend Larry Campbell
 who calls again three months later and wants you
 to once again read "that quiche thing."
After all, it is the season to be thankful
 but I suspect the real reason he calls
 is because it had his name in it.
And this is for the offhand way he mentions,
 "Wouldn't it be kinda neat to write a sequel to that poem?"

But that's OK,
 for one of the things I can be thankful for is that
 this time my good friend Larry calls two weeks ahead

and I have plenty of time to mull over
 the many blessings in my life
 regardless of the fact
 that I wait until the night before to write them down.

For if I just take the time to notice
 two weeks of time echoes again and again
 with reminders of the blessings of my life.

Shelby drops by for dinner
 and her presence in my home resounds with reminders
 that my own childhood was free from fear
 and filled with comfort and love and security.

I go to Ladies' Bible Study
    and that hour and 15 minutes resounds with affirmation
    that I have friends that will laugh with me
    and cry with me and lift me up in prayer
    when I don't have a clue as to how to pray for myself.

I come home from school and sit down to dinner
    with a husband who tells me stories of funny things
    my 18-month-old son did that day.
    Where did he learn to open the cabinet,
    turn on the cassette player,
    rip the eject door off,
    and put his tongue up against the rolling heads?
    And dinner resounds with laughter,
    and our home echoes with joy.

My mother calls to remind me
    that on December 7 my grandparents
    will celebrate their 70th wedding anniversary,
    and that call resounds with memories of cousins
    tucked in beds and cots and rollaways
    upstairs in the old farmhouse
    listening as our grandparents' nightly prayers
    drift up through the vents.
    We hold our breath and listen for each of our names
    as God is asked to keep His guiding hand on us.
    And even 600 miles away
    I still hear the echoes of a legacy of generations
    devoted to God
    Telling me the greatest thing I can do for my children
    is to teach them to love God
    by loving God myself.

And as we celebrate a holiday that celebrates
    God's many blessings,
    May I always take the time to stop and listen
    to the echoes of those many blessings
    that resound through all my days.

An Easter Story

I keep telling my 11th-grade literature students
    that we humans don't know very many stories.
    We just keep telling the same ones over and over again.
And when we hit on a *really* good story
    one that seeps into our bones,
    keeps the rhythm with our hearts,
    and echoes the music of the spheres,
    We tell that story again and again and again.

Here's a really good story:
    Once upon a time,
    out of death came life.

We've told the story again and again.
We heard it from the Egyptians on the banks of the Nile:
    The beautiful, lone Phoenix rises
    out of the ashes of the fire that consumed it.

Margery Williams called it "The Velveteen Rabbit":
    A boy's love for the shabby, well-worn stuffed bunny
    is so profound that he's transformed on the trash heap
    and made *real*.

John Steinbeck told us the story in *Of Mice and Men*:

    George loves his friend, the big, bumbling idiot Lennie,
        and has the courage to transport Lennie
        with a bullet to the head
        from a world of confusion and danger
        to one where he can have his own place

and feed the rabbits
and "live off the fatta the land."

Out of death came life.

And here's the very best part:

AND THE STORY BECAME A MAN AND LIVED AMONG US.

What a story it was when He lived it,
    banishing death with every step
    and bringing life
        to lepers (or AIDS victims)
        to tax collectors (or mob-connected bookies)
        to harlots (or hookers—some themes are
            timeless)

It's all the stuff best-selling novels are made of.

When he got to that Lazarus bit, I'm sure the movie of-
    fers were through the roof. And that was just a
    rough draft.

Who would've guessed that the pain and sorrow and
    darkness and terror and betrayal and disappoint-
    ment and all-encompassing, smothering DEATH of
    Friday would be catapulted into a sparkling, laugh-
    ing, angels-dancing morning of LIFE on Sunday.

Now THAT'S a final revision.

Tell the story.

The Legacy

I was 29 years old before I lost a grandparent. And besides passing on to me genes of longevity, they provided me a heritage of faith and love and stability. Both sets of my grandparents are simple people who know where true worth lies. Unlike me, they don't have so much "stuff" that distracts them from living. When my paternal grandfather died in 1986, I realized that this simple farmer had added to my life a dimension I would have missed without him. You see, I have lived my entire life in large metropolitan areas. I like it that way. But I also worry if my kids will grow up with a void that should be filled by the smell of dirt, the shiny place the hoe makes on your hand, the dinner plate filled with stuff you grew yourself. I will try as best I can (perhaps two tomato plants at a time) to pass on to my children the legacy my grandpa left me. I wrote the following poem and read it at the funeral service of R. Bryan Staples, 1897—1986.

Memories flood back sharp and strong
    in times of mourning such as these.
And I see once again a man—
A man who loved his God, his family,
    and his land.
The legacy he leaves me is a rich one
    of images I treasure
    as he treasured the richness
    of God's creation.

Grandpa,
    You leave me the early-morning mist
      on fertile fields

I've seen through the upstairs window
of a house still wrapped in sleep.
You leave me a solitary figure in familiar overalls
between the rows of garden greenery
gathering what God had kissed with sweetness.

I have a legacy of memories of a grandpa
taking two granddaughters on tractor rides—
what a treat for city kids!
I'd sit on the tool box;
Karen would balance on the fender. Remember?
And when the ride was over,
we'd circle the pond and laugh out loud
as frogs went plop, plop into the water,
scared by our laughter.

You leave me the summer
when a 7-year-old and a 10-year-old
"helped" you plant the garden.
You didn't seem to mind when
the box of peas was spilled;
You laughed when a huge clump of vines
grew in the middle of the neat row.

You leave me the sounds of sitting
in the old familiar swing
at dawn or dusk or hot afternoons
listening to the birds sing:
What was that, Grandpa? A bobwhite.
And that? A cardinal.
And that one? A whippoorwill.
We'd listen hard for the whippoorwills.

Images flood my mind
of the rich heritage that is mine.
A heritage of loving the land,
of reverence for life,
of a respect for nature,
of worshiping in awe
this great earth's Maker.

I mourn the passing of this life
  and this way of life;
   of living so close to God's handiwork
   that day by day you see life and growth
    repeat itself again and again.

I mourn the fact that children I may have
  will have no one to teach them
  this love of the land that you've taught me.

But I am comforted by this legacy you leave me—
  this love of the earth and things that grow.
For, Grandpa, somewhere back in time,
  perhaps in my simple childhood mind,
  you, as a man,
  became quite similar to God's great land.

And as we give you back to earth,
The earth, in turn, gives you back to me.
For when I see the morning mist
  on rich green fertile fields,
  or see a bullfrog jump,
  or listen, listen very hard for a whippoorwill,
Once again, you will be with me.